Lane Changes

ALSO BY DAVID LAWRENCE

Boxer Rebellion

Steel Toe Boots

Dementia Pugilistica

Blame It on the Scientists (Chapbook)

Lane Changes

poems

David Lawrence

Four Way Books
Tribeca / New York City

Distributed by
University Press of New England
Hanover and London

Editorial Office
Four Way Books
POB 535, Village Station
New York, NY 10014
www.fourwaybooks.com

Library of Congress Cataloging-in-Publication Data

Lawrence, David, 1947-
Lane changes : poems / David Lawrence.
p. cm.
ISBN-13: 978-1-884800-79-5 (pbk. : acid-free paper)
ISBN-10: 1-884800-79-3 (pbk. : acid-free paper)
I. Title.
PS3562.A9117D34 2007
811'.54--dc22
2007018779

This book is manufactured in the United States of America. Four Way Books is a not-for-profit literary press. We are grateful for the assistance we receive from individual donors, public arts agencies, and private foundations.

This publication is made possible with public funds from the New York State Council on the Arts, a state agency.

State of the Arts
NYSCA

Distributed by University Press of New England
One Court Street, Lebanon, NH 03766

[clmp]
We are a proud member of the Council of Literary Magazines and Presses.

2nd printing, 2017

CONTENTS

WHITE PLAINS

I remember getting hit so hard in the head
That the gray canvas turned into
An albino snowstorm.
I was wandering through the drifts
Looking for the abominable
Snowman.
I couldn't find him until he hit me
Again.
I didn't know Puerto Ricans
Liked Alaska.
He was wearing red, white and blue
Shorts with one star.
He chased me through a snow bank.
Good thing I had my snow
Shoes on.
I turned around
And hit him under the chin
With a frozen hand.
That was the first fight I ever won
With an uppercut.
It's a sophisticated punch,
You know.
Like Gray Goose vodka.
I was so dizzy that night I couldn't find
My igloo.
I wanted attention so much that I boxed
My head off.
The neighbors didn't even notice me
Sneaking through their backyards.

ACTING LESSONS

Do not imagine that I am not a star just because I am ignored like a stone in the Gobi Desert. No one knows you till you have all the paraphernalia, fanfare, disputations and groupies gasping for breath. Not that it should matter. But I feel like I am dancing on a giant screen that condenses my little bravados into turning points. And the sequels flow like popcorn from some celestial machine so that I am airborne in a flimflam sequence of frames. I am discovering the pleasure of burning my own hand on an imaginary match head. And this delusion of fame roller blades around the corner, seating itself on a bench in front of me. I see myself astounding the Hollywood sky like a sweet tart.

METROPOLIS

Your tickets to the ballet insult me. Opera is a migraine. I sit on the edge of the world with a stick poking holes in your Master's degree. Then you put on a strip tease that turns the afternoon to denim high jinks. I admit that you have intelligent skin. And your ass has a lot to say. Later we walk behind a bus to show we support mass transit. The streetlamps come out during the afternoon to bring on the feeling of night. At the hot dog stand there is frolic in the mustard. A caterpillar in the park is smoking hash. Did I invent you to imagine me?

UNLIMITED DETENTION

I have fallen from the face of the universe like a stuffed nose. Sometimes I can't breathe amongst all this failure. If I could break your ankle I would buy you a new sock to hide the bone. I danced with my own terror like I wasn't afraid of strange girls. Rejection is a broken erector set. You can't build on the sadness of toys. You didn't want to see my bloated face, musing from the beer can. In school they used to put me in detention because the teachers liked to keep me around. I was a hang glider in my own delinquent levitation. I am still up in the sky looking down.

NIGHTY

I turn off all the lights and play black out.
I swear I won't turn my flashlight on.
I wash myself with dark soap.
I am the inner tube
In blackness's tire.
I feel the whites in my eyes
Turning on me like Sammy the Bull.
I put on shades.
If I could only disappear into a fist
I'd know what it is to be a team
Of knuckles.

INSURING MADISON EQUITIES

I asked Fred if he had bound the umbrella
On Madison Equities yet.
"You're not going to believe it,"
He said.
"What?"
"I'm charging the client seven hundred
Thousand dollars,"
He said.
"It only cost me thirty grand
To place at Reliance."
"You're nuts," I said.
He was stealing too much.
I was nervous.
I wanted to wade in the river of theft
With rubber fishing boots.
I wanted a condom for my business
Fucking.
This was mad.
"That's all the company wanted.
What was I to do?
Give away your money, boss?"
I loved when he called me boss.
"Someone's going to do it for less
Than our seven hundred thousand,"
I said.
"Who? The losses stink,"
He said.
"Then how'd you get it done?" I asked.
"That's for me to know," he said.
That's why I paid him so much.

He sheltered me.
Business with him was on a need-
To-know basis.
And he stole for me more
Than he stole from me.
"We could go to jail for overcharging
So much.
You got no restraint.
Even thieves have a sense of proportion,"
I said.
"What proportion?
You can't be partly pregnant.
It's done,"
Fred said.
I visualized a baby with hundred-dollar
Bills pasted all over his body.
He was a green ball
Of Benjamin Franklins.
He represented a hundred lies.
He was a piggy bank
And I was the piggy.
Let it pass as all things pass.
I couldn't turn down a risk already taken.
How could I lose?
Fred was doing all the stealing.
It was for my company.
I got the money.
He did the work.

Of course I'd take care of him.
Pay the Pied Piper or he steals your children.
I'd buy him a new car
Or pay for a bunch of hormone shots
For his lover's sex change
Operation.
Life imitates art.
This was the real *Dog Day Afternoon.*
I felt like I was walking with an umbrella
Under the rain.
I had piles of hundred-dollar bills
Hidden under my poncho.
Was I a bandito?
This was not the first time
I was singing in the rain.
I wasn't an American in Paris.
I was Paris in the American.
I was sinister like the Left Bank.
Only it wasn't raining.
The greenbacks were dry and I salivated
Over money that fell on me
Like a sun shower.
I had a dry sense of humor.
I wouldn't cry about the jail sentence
Down the road.
I was amused.
I could take punishment.
But a decade later I was not amusé
By the French who stabbed

Us in the back
With their interest in oil wells in Iraq.
Is politics a crime?
How do we send a nation to jail?
I suddenly hated Gene Kelly.
I wasn't moldy like French bread.
But I was penicillin for my allies
In crime.
I ate punishments for Fred and Steve
Who betrayed me.
I was not a hero.
I did not sit on a grenade.
I just wasn't built for snitching.
I bunkered down with integrity like a soldier
Even though I looked like a thief.

POET AND BUSINESSMAN AND…

Well, there were precedents.
Wallace Stevens.
The critics make me laugh.
They think he was a big shot.
I spent more on clothes than he earned.
He wallowed in middle management's
Wide waist like a belt.
I hired and fired insurance men
Like Stevens.
T.S. Eliot was not a CEO.
Bankers lack imagination.
There's no money in banking
Unless you're the bank.
I owned a whole floor on Wall Street.
I had offices in three states.
I'd buy ten Armani suits at a time.
I gave Hermès ties to doormen
To hang themselves.
I was a boxer too.
You wouldn't have believed it in the title
So I just wrote, "Poet and Businessman and…."
I liked to write and fight.
I hated the puny Jew bosses
Who yelled at their
Ex-athlete flunkies
And used employment as a carrot
And a stick.
Hey, hold on, I'm a Jew.
But I didn't boss around my big dumb
Catholic workers, huddling

Around the copying machine
Hoping they weren't
Duplicate.
I was never cheap.
I let my salesmen steal from me.
I banked on the kindness of my strangeness.
I was a branch of fresh air.

THE BUSINESS OF DYING

When I close a deal
I am king.
When I lose an account
I am loss.
This life is about loss
And the lessons
I learn from being broke
Prepare me
For death.
I am learning how
To lose my breath
While still inhaling air
From death's
Aqualung.
It's not the tank that empties.
I am full of myself
While dying.
It is the unfairness
Of the Deep Sea Diver who
Put me in this body
Suit.
I am severely agnostic.

CANCER DANCE

"It's a good cause." Who said that?
They're all thinking it.
Spinach is good for you too but
I don't eat it.
I don't want to be Popeye.
I'd have to let out my sleeves
To fit my forearms.
Why does my wife make me come
Here each year?
A room full of rich people gambling
And donating their losses
To death.
I never liked to dance.
I do a fox trot with my wife.
She is civilization.
I am an ax chopping down the slow trees
Of giving.
There is selfishness in her open hand.
I think she wants to pick
At my fingers.
Don't talk to me about social events.
Hussein would take out your tongue.
These words once held saliva.
I brush.
I clean it all up.
The cancer authorities let us write off
Our gambling debts.
We bought gifts from Cartier
And Tiffany's
And deducted them as charitable contributions.

Hi Kenny,
Nice tuxedo you've got on.
Right, a cowboy tie and pink
Ruffles.
Hello Steve,
Are you as rich as you say you are?
He wears a creased hundred-dollar bill in place
Of his pocket hankie.
Barbara,
Are you still planning to live in the Rain
Forest and help the rain?
A forest green Ungaro dress
Spiced by dog shit on her pumps.
I was never a charitable person.
Fake is not the imprimatur
Of a good upbringing.
Is it oxymoronic tomfoolery
Or a dance for
Cancer?
I am the homeless man
For the MTA ad.
Art wanders around with a tin cup.
I hate what I pose for.

STEVE K

You were wired that night at the Japanese Restaurant.
You looked like tuna wrapped in seaweed.
Your hands were at your sides
Like you were pickpocketing yourself.

You kept asking leading questions
Like a jockey pulling
On our bridles.

Fred and I thought you were taping us
But we were afraid to rip
Off your shirt.
It wouldn't be polite.
The Japanese are ceremonial like tea.

We hardly revealed anything about our crimes.
But the Feds are information whores.
They are always looking for reasons
To bend over.
When you gave them the tapes
They spread their cheeks and took three years
Off your sentence.

Just to show they are professionals
They sent us to Schuylkill Federal Prison Camp.

LAUNDERER

After I stole fifty thousand dollars in cash
I went for a walk in the South Street Seaport.

The air was clean
And the sea
Was salt,
Lapping near the boutiques
And my felonious Wall Street.

I bumped into crime, himself,
John Gotti
And his bodyguard walking
Past Sloppy Louie's.

I know I had more hundred-dollar bills
In my attaché case than he did.
I wanted to say,
"John, I'm the man."
But why get competitive with a psychopath.

POPS

I stole a million dollars from the IRS
And they gave me two years.
Nice gift.
Good accommodations in the Poconos.
Canned ham from Desert Storm,
Dibs on the lower bunk
After a year.

I miss those days,
Communing with the junior mafia,
Discussing sales techniques
With the drug dealers,
Computer crime with the hackers.
A little old man,
Pops,
Was there on welfare fraud.
What was that?
A dollar ninety-eight cent crime?

At night
Pops couldn't make it to the urinal
And would piss
On the floor.
One of the bikers wanted to stick his nose
In the puddle like a dog.
He didn't.
I wasn't looking for trouble.
If he did
What would I have done?
Punched the biker?
Or made fun of sweet, little old Pops barking?

EVANDER HOLYFIELD WON'T RETIRE

It's not about the money.
It's about how good it feels to get hit
Up the side of the head.
And you standing there in your naked pain
While the audience peeks
At you
Whacking off to how you take the hurt
So good.
Is it worth the slurred speech
And forgetting what you are saying
In the middle of each
Sentence?
Your actions are your answer.
You sign up for more.
You want to bleed like Christ
Hanging half-naked before a crowd
Of laughter.
You are *L'Etranger.*
You mistake curses for affirmations.
It's not about the shekels.
Where else can you make a statement
And be heard?
The echo has a face.
Your injuries are a form of dialogue with loneliness.
Your fighting past your prime
Is like a dirty old man flirting with the skirts.

JOB'S COUSIN

On the other side of wandering there's a clubfoot.
I can't go anywhere without my limp.
What does a rabbit foot
Have to do with winter?
Nothing.
I am looking for luck.
Good.
I'll never find it.
According to my birth certificate I am related
To Job.
I get a lot of boils when I'm mad.
Sometimes I'm nuts like soft water.
I'm going to float out of here
And find death's lotion.

VAN GOGH

I would speak into your ear if you hadn't cut it off.
"Nice paintings," I'd say.
I've fallen for hookers too.
But the suicide,
There's where you screwed up.
I hurt myself for attention.
When you're dead you don't know who's looking.
Unless you're such a cocky bastard
You believe in heaven.

NOT CLAUDE REINS

Neither am I Humphrey Bogart.
But I do find myself in the movie *Casablanca.*
It's drizzling.
The night smells of jasmine and fucked up
Romances.
I am not Ingrid Bergman.

I am the binocular unhappiness that stalks
The tarmac beneath the airplane wheels,
Slicking up,
Hoping the plane doesn't make it off the runway.

DOWN BY THE OCEAN

What's left behind also goes forward, dragged
Behind the hunchback's foot.
Tomorrow carries yesterday like a lifeguard
Carrying a child out of the water
Onto the beach where it is stared at
As an accident
Rather than something to look forward to
Beneath the beach umbrellas.
I go back down to the water
And put my head
In a wave
To practice drowning,
To do the backstroke on a sand castle like
The crush of God.
It's the old accidental religion that inspires undertow.

CONFUSION OF WATER

The last time the refulgence of rain detected
Thirst in the windows
I was in my room talking to myself
As I was artfully dodging who I was.
These times
Come and go but loneliness
Is a chronic
Condition.
Even when your lips touch me,
When you stand there staring at me with glacial hips,
I begin
To worry about the dirty rain
Falling
On my nose against the glass.

SOLITARY

I was found turning a steering wheel
In the playpen.
Don't follow me.
I got away in a stolen car.

If I could be a child again
I would be my own son because I am as lax
As nitrous oxide
And as loving as a look the other way.

CALVARY HOSPITAL

for Mom

If you live forever it is not long enough
So what you have left is nothing at the hospice
And disease is a chronic band-aid I'd like to slap
Over my mouth to silence hope
And distractions.
It's going down real bad in this hospital
Like a jack sticking into a child's knee.
When I was young and a dog attacked me
You chased it with a bowl of spinach.
How many pick up sticks do I have to give you
To give the whole game back.
I respect your pain like literature.
There is a beautiful dialect in your tumor.
I walked on a tightrope
To see if I could fall into your disease.
But your suffering is the loneliness of Jell-O.
It shakes.
I will listen for your advice in my chest.
There will be somebody sitting in your absence.
I will unwrap your hand from its box
And hold it when you are gone.

IT'S HARD TO CELEBRATE YOUR HEAD

Write your name on my arm
If you want to be part of me like that afternoon.
When you rolled down the grassy knoll
I was there to catch your brains in my dream
Of assassination.
There are so many deaths it's hard to celebrate your head,
Shattered like peanut shells.
That was a long time ago and by now you'd be dead without the shots.
We come and we go and then we don't come anymore
Which is all about remembering your solid face.
Not that I ever gave a damn about a President.
I like real people like my brother
And the way that he thinks it matters if the sun rises,
The morning engenders frosted flakes.
The only thing that makes me angry is your ghost.

THE CHOCOLATE SHOPS OF MADISON AVENUE

I will never be able to walk away from you.
The daisies in the park are forgotten,
The dog shit hardens, crusts,
Lingers.
I go for walks with your shadow but it's not enough.
I strain my neck looking for you.
There are chalk marks in the sky
Where your spirit fell as if at a police crime scene.
I want to knock a cop from his horse,
Sprout wings and fly to your soul's body bag.

DARKROOM

Ask me once again and I'll tell you no.
It's easier.
I can't fall in love when
I have a good sense of balance
And I don't know what
Love is.
It is mysterious like God.
It's a lack of definition.
It is a darkroom affair.
Just me and the chemicals.
You come out photographic.
I am embarrassed to look at you naked
And the developing is not
Easy.
I put a bra on my eyes.
I need support.
I'm not going anywhere with these negatives.

RETIRED

I gave up sex at forty-six when I went to jail.
I wanted to be able to tell Bubba,
"I'm just not into that shit."
But Bubba was just not into me.
He cozied up to the little black drag queen
Who used his sock as a pocketbook.
"Hey, what am I, chopped liver?"
I wanted to say.
Am I crazy?
Was I jealous?
I didn't want Bubba.
I just wanted freedom.
Not from jail.
I liked the lack of responsibility.
But from my sex drive
Which in the compulsions of youth
Had parked me in vacant lots
Where jealous ladies
Wanted to flatten my tires and make it look
Like they had company in the winter in the Hamptons
When all their neighbors had gone to Florida.

THE CORRECTNESS OF MISTAKES

To read the marginalia of your life
You must wander outside
Of the text
And pluck truths from the holes punched
In your blue lines.

I get old.
I've done it wrong.
First the balance goes and then the desire.

I lie down on the beach and pretend I am a mollusk
Waiting to celebrate my reincarnation
At high tide.

KID TOWN

In a party of cartoon faces
I wondered why I was an adult.
What was I doing with so many handfuls
Of years?
The kids looked at me like a fist.
As sad as my whiskers
Were the shouts of surprise.
Children's stories don't end.
The hurt goes on beyond Bambi's
Death
And sometimes I'm so happy
I remember
When I'd see an elephant fly.

MORE TIME

In prison they take gambling debts seriously. The dirty cop said, "I don't have to pay." The drug dealers beat him over the head with dumbbells. There was a tinny sound. I saw the pool of blood in the stairway and felt nostalgic. The ring in Gleason's Boxing Gym was always spattered with red dots like a Jackson Pollock painting. An artist paints with a palette in his veins. They carried the dirty cop across the field and put him in a van. We never saw him again. I heard that he got brain damage. Big deal. He wasn't very smart. The C.O.'s put thirty people in isolation. They questioned everyone until they gathered enough lies. Eight people never came back from the hole. No one escaped from prison but a lot of people kept disappearing. How many extra years did the attackers get? In what other joints? I remember T.J. He was a tall black guy with teeth like a grille. I liked him. His eyes beamed like headlamps when he laughed. His life fell off the curb when he attempted to murder the cop. They should have given the badge more time for making T.J. mad.

NEGATIVE FROND

All around the garden the walls are falling in so that the tulips can escape. The knees of the statue touch the ground and I bless its stony prayer. I can't get out of this place because this place isn't here. On the other side of the river lies New Jersey. That's a kick in the groin. I'd rather look up to Connecticut.

HANDICAPPED BUS

It takes the driver five minutes to load the bus.
It's a wheelchair party.
The masses shouldn't wait for the few.
I'd let you eat cake.
Watch you roll.
I am democratic.
I hate the handicapped.
I am disabled.
It is only mental.
My body works like the cha-cha.
You are parked next to me.
Your features are eroded,
Whacked smooth,
Winded.
I want to play baseball with your nose.
The driver gets back into his seat,
Feeling like the Red Cross.
I am not looking to win brownie points
Or merit badges.
I was kicked out of the cub scouts
For selling firecrackers without fuses.
Your legs are duds.
I don't have time for failures.
I ride at half-fare.
It takes three lithium pills to stop the urge
To steal your wheelchair.

PUNCHING OUT LEOR

It's not nice to hit your student.
I'm the only trainer at Gleason's Gym
Who likes to do it.
            Leor is heavier than I am
And can bench three hundred pounds.
He's less than half my age.
I'm fifty-seven,

A little old to be playing tuff guy.
I'll kill you.
I'll kill your mother.
The angry voices are heady in my head.

I have minor brain damage so
I tell Leor not to hit me
In the head.
He has heavy hands.
If he belted me in the temple
            I'd become religious,
            Stupid,
An overturned moneychanger's table.
But the rules are in my favor.
I fight with my hands down.
I don't even cover my face.

I land an uppercut that is as beautiful
As the air around the Matterhorn;
It's loose like powder
And drifts into his chin with no muscle
Tension,
A skier's stop,

A swimmer's punch,
A bull's deathblow.

Then I catch him in the ribs
With a boomerang,
My hand snapping back so fast
To show him
Where I come from and where
                    He's going.

He stops.
I tell him,
"We're friends so it doesn't matter
if you stop. But if you're in a real
fight and your opponent sees you're
hurt he'll get excited and kill you."

Friendly advice from the wise old man.
Leor thanks me.
He learned something.
He gives me twenty-five dollars
For the lesson.
I learned something too.
          I'm young.
                    I'm alive.
                              I'm still a real
          Motherfucker.

WHY I BOX

You hit me. It feels like affection.
My head is numb.
There is nothing in it but a quarry where
I hear myself cry.

When my mother hit me I laughed.
It didn't hurt.
Love is funny.
I miss her hand slapping after me
As I ran down the stairs
From my bedroom to the living room
Where my dad grabbed me
And gave me a slug for my mother,
For love.

Knock me out.
It's a way of getting close to you,
Of sharing death with another human being,
Or lying down with my birth scream.
Life and death come and go like rounds.
When you hit the floor,
I'll date the ring card girl.

AT THE BOXING CLINIC

In the land of the brain-damaged old pros
A clear thought is lost.
We are a club.
Merry fellows.
All the anger beaten out of us.
Once I was a snowflake,
A winter dandelion.
I was as rich as a drift
And lost as a dollar in a field
Of fortunate twenties
Without money clips to keep them down.
Now I am poor as a dip in the road.
At the bottom of our careers
We are here to get our licenses
As trainers,
To work the corners of amateurs,
Jealous of their broken noses,
Their glories.
The eyes in our beat up faces
Carry the sadness of elephants
Wandering around graveyards
Not yet ready to buy plots.
The bags on our cheeks are suitcases.
We are all going nowhere.

FOUR ROUND FIGHTER

I'm a first time pro, a novice at death.
Between rounds I wonder what I'm doing here.
As a kid I got hit with my mom's belt.
Who didn't?
It was entertainment. Learning how
To bob and weave.
Do I like to take chances?
Or do chances like to take me up up
On a raft above Niagara Falls.
I attempt suicide.
I am in over my head.
I look at my corpse and discover that I am alive.
I have fish in my veins.
I swim with my boxing gloves on.
I pull myself up on the ring ropes.
Boxing is my life preserver.
Punching is a beautiful way to hurt the sun.
When it shines on me
I knock its teeth out.
I am afraid of Halloween.
I am the pumpkin.
I am your pie.
It's not about winning or losing.
It's about how much you can take
While still going forward.
I'm still standing.
I give you my candle to light your way home.

SON

I can't get over how you look like me and perhaps you are me in the corners of odd thoughts that have my etchings on them. A few years back I believed the buck stopped here but now I see there is something going down a bloodline in a genetic canoe. So that I no longer need to live or hang around because you are going west, scalping light from disasters, making braided utterances. It's nice to wake up in the morning dead and know that you are alive for me, listening to the birds chirping and waiting for events to rise from their beds and happen. I hope you think of me sometimes. I'll be the dead man bobbing to the lake's surface in your face.

HUGS COOPERATE

When we went swimming in the naked mountain lake above dispensation,
We weren't really there but I was imagining your long draft
Squeezing the ripples from the water and your cool lips
Slipping like a tray of ice cubes.
There were so many things that never happened that are real
And the clock ticking is a pendulum that flicks like a tongue.
In the center of burnt toast the butter slid down the knife
Like nostalgia for stale investigations and commensurate twattle.
I loved the queen of hearts among all the other playing cards, flipped.
On your lap I used to build sand castles to teach your groin
Lessons about the beach falling on redundant horns.
I am startled by the beach ball's notes
And the music of crabs swishing through the undertow like saliva.
Where are we going when the fist fight of the future
Has rejected our compromise?
I cannot put aside the interminable friction of naïve smooches
And the way hugs cooperate with your appeal.
I want to stay with you for as long as an invitation.

MATADOR

Everyone tells me you are impossible like a cake with missing slices
Or a plastic bag with holes carrying water and a goldfish.
I am the only one in the world who ice-skates on the equator
And says he loves the way you are picked on
Like a nose.
The worse you get the more your dress lifts around your thighs
And the scrub brush washes the stains
From my ambivalent tongue.
Don't meet me at the bull stadium
Because the fans will insist I stick a pole in your shoulder
And cut off your ear.
I scratch at you like you are my personal itch.
You should not drown yourself in the bathtub
Because your life is precious as a medicine cabinet.
When you are not looking I pull banana slices
From your underwear.
I rubbed a piece of pink quartz and came.
You could be tasteful if you weren't so much like a finger pointing.
In the valley of goulash I found that you were a stew I could digest
Along with the peppers and cucumbers
And it wasn't that you were too spiced and jumbled for others
But I had the good taste to see you as simmered
And petite.

HAVANA & PARAKEETS

It's not the effort that fouls the cigar.
I smoke your lungs out.
Love is a little funny thing
Like a bird.
I hang from the dowel
And swing back
And forth.
I wish I could get out of this cage
So that I could pull wheat
From the sky and make
Our relationship
Whole.
I could butter us up.
I could lather us with a knife.

SOUTHAMPTON

I am battling with polo ponies. Someone has stolen the corner from the street so that I can't change direction. The dress you were wearing was superficial. I have forgotten my intentions. You belong among the mansions and the unread books. A light rain disagrees with the sun. When I mingle with your friends I feel like I am in solitary confinement. I take out a picture of you and argue with it.

DANCING WITH INSULTS

I heard what you were saying.
Not a word.
Just the music of your critique.
It was something
About me and a suck face.
And then screeches.
Were the screeches insults?
Perhaps you called me a fuck butt
Or a wiseass?
How should I know?
I heard the rhythm.
There was a word or two
I recognized.
And I wanted to dance.
I wanted to move in and out of all
The bad things you might
Have said.

FRIENDS

I once walked a horse through a field in the rain
And felt her warm wet body in my palm
Wanting to read my future
In her horse hairs
But happy enough to know that I was bridled
To her journey.
In the barn I told her that I loved her,
Brushed her and fed her oats.
If I never touch you again
I will always be walking you though some wet field.

BROKEN SHOULDER

There are things I don't want to say that are said.
The meaning of that innuendo is plain.
I don't know what I mean
But I am becoming all of the implications.
I lie down with wheat
And become your bowl of cereal.
I am the silence and I am the swallowed word.
I am a goat eating cans.
I am the broken shoulder of a line
In a discarded poem.
A doctor puts me in a sling.
I am the taped elbow of all the words I ever slung.

FIELDING

Someone stole the field from the high school.
I was happy I no longer had to play gym.
Until the teacher put us in the boiler room
And tossed hot coals around like our futures.
I didn't know that I'd end up a bum.
If I did I would have caught that punk
Who stole the field
And returned it to the field.
I would have fielded in that field.
I would have cherished a lot of field.

OLD WEST LAKE DRIVE

It is what is missing that makes me resent the parking meters
That fine me for not having a car.
It is not summer yet.
Spring comes around the corner in a braless woman.
I never liked my home in Montauk.
Why do I want to go there?
It is no longer mine.
I walk around New York feeling like I was sold.
Even the winter is gone.
The snow has traveled to the North Pole to look for a job
During the off-season.
I have a hunch that death is like this,
Finding my bicycle on my old front lawn
Where I am now trespassing.

ACKNOWLEDGMENTS

Art: Mag: "It's Hard to Celebrate Your Head"(appeared as "Dallas")
Barbaric Yawp: "Handicapped Bus," "Poet and Businessman and..."
Bathtub Gin: "Why I Box"
By Line: "Broken Shoulder"
California State Poetry Society Poetry Letter and Literary Review: "Confusion of Water"
Caveat Lector: "Pops"
Chiron Review: "Dancing with Insults," "Darkroom"
88: A Journal of Contemporary Poetry: "Not Claude Reins"
Epicenter: "Cancer Dance"
Folio: "Acting Lessons"
Green Hills Literary Lantern: "Kid Town," "Punching Out Leor"
Hawaii Review: "Fielding" (appeared as "Career,") and "Metropolis"
Hiram Poetry Review: "Retired"
Hunger: "Unlimited Detention" (appeared as "Bourgeois Clock")
Kimera: "Matador"
The Laurel Review: "More Time"
Main Street Rag: "Launderer" and "Steve K"(appeared as "Marc K")
Mankato: "Havana & Parakeets," "Job's Cousin"
Mudfish: "Son," "Calvary Hospital"
Nanny Fanny: "Holyfield Won't Retire"
Nimrod: "Four Round Fighter"
96 Inc.: "Old West Lake Drive"
North American Review: "At the Boxing Clinic"
Pearl: "The Chocolate Shops of Madison Avenue"
Poesy: "Solitary" (appeared as "Lacking Discipline")
Poetry Depth Quarterly: "Friends"
Porcupine Magazine: "Hugs Cooperate"
Pudding Magazine: "Down by the Ocean"
Skidrow Penthouse: "Southampton," "Van Gogh," "Insuring Madison Equities"
The South Carolina Review: "Nighty"
Straw Dog: "White Plains"
Underwood Review: "Negative Frond"

David Lawrence has a Ph.D. in literature from CUNY Graduate Center and taught at Hunter College. In 1976 he went into business and within five years became the CEO of several large insurance brokerages on Wall Street. During that time, he became a professional boxer and fought on television in venues like Vegas and Atlantic City. He made a movie of his fight career, "Boxer Rebellion," which played at the Sundance Film Festival. In 1993 he didn't pay his taxes on a few of his accounts, losing his multimillion-dollar businesses and ending up doing a two-year bid in a Federal Prison Camp. Prior to, during and subsequent to jail he became a rapper and did three albums. He has been married since 1972 and lives with his wife, Lauren, in New York City. He has a 27-year-old son, Graham. He writes every day. He teaches boxing at Gleason's Gym in Brooklyn. He joyfully believes he has the perfect life—writing and fighting.